The Aztec Empire

LOUISE SPILSBURY

raintree
a Capstone company — publishers for children

Raintree is an imprint of Capstone Global Library Limited, a company incorporated in England and Wales having its registered office at 264 Banbury Road, Oxford, OX2 7DY – Registered company number: 6695582

www.raintree.co.uk
myorders@raintree.co.uk

Original illustrations © Capstone Global Library Limited 2020
Originated by Capstone Global Library Ltd
Printed and bound in India

ISBN 978 1 4747 7774 2 (hardback)
ISBN 978 1 4747 7783 4 (paperback)

British Library Cataloguing in Publication Data
A full catalogue record for this book is available from the British Library.

Acknowledgements
We would like to thank the following for permission to reproduce photographs: Cover: Shutterstock: Fer Gregory: bottom; Elena Fernandez Z: top; Inside: Flickr: Dennis Jarvis CC BY-SA 2.0: pp. 32–33; Shutterstock: Carlos.araujo: p. 10; Everett Historical: p. 45b; Diego Grandi: p. 9b; Macrowildlife: p. 13; Mistervlad: pp. 1, 27b; Sari Oneal: p. 41b; TravelNerd: pp. 22–23; Cezary Wojtkowski: pp. 4–5, 26–27; Wikimedia Commons: pp. 4t, 4b, 18–19, 36–37; John Carter Brown Library: pp. 5b, 12, 17; Simon Burchell: pp. 23r, 35l; Margaret Duncan Coxhead: p. 11; Manuel Parada López de Corselas: p. 43; Antonio de Solís (author), artist unidentified: p. 25r; Juan de Tovar: pp. 24–25, 30, 31, 38, 40–41; The Field Museum Library: pp. 6–7; Geni: p. 29b; Dr. Bernd Gross: p. 37r; Hans Hillewaert: pp. 33r, 42; Ignote, codex from 16th century: pp. 28–29; Emanuel Leutze: pp. 44–45; Madman2001: p. 39; Purchase 2015 Benefit Fund and Lila Acheson Wallace Gift, 2016: p. 15; Rama: p. 16; Diego Rivera: pp. 8–9; Wolfgang Sauber: p. 19br; Vassil: p. 21r; Xjunajpu: pp. 34–35; Z-m-k: pp. 20–21; Zuchinni one: p. 7r.

Every effort has been made to contact copyright holders of material reproduced in this book. Any omissions will be rectified in subsequent printings if notice is given to the publisher.

All the internet addresses (URLs) given in this book were valid at the time of going to press. However, due to the dynamic nature of the internet, some addresses may have changed, or sites may have changed or ceased to exist since publication. While the author and publisher regret any inconvenience this may cause readers, no responsibility for any such changes can be accepted by either the author or the publisher.

Contents

CHAPTER 1

Empire of blood

The unstoppable Aztecs used violence and war to **conquer** their neighbours and take control of large areas of land. This powerful **civilization** built and ruled a vast, often cruel, **empire** in central and southern Mexico that lasted from the 1400s to the early 1500s.

It was no wonder that other **tribes** living in Mexico at that time hated and feared the Aztecs. The Aztecs were dangerous warriors. Every Aztec man was trained to fight ferociously and capture enemies in battle.

The Aztecs believed in human **sacrifice**. They held special ceremonies in which they slowly killed innocent people simply to please their gods.

Aztec **priests** wore terrifying masks when they carried out sinister sacrifices.

DEADLY DID YOU KNOW?

The Aztecs roamed for years hoping to see an eagle eating its prey on a cactus. They believed this would be a sign from a god showing them where to settle. When they finally saw it, they built their first city there.

This image shows the Aztecs witnessing an eagle eating its **prey** on top of a cactus.

5

Brutal battles

The Aztecs did not fight to kill in all of their battles. They often went to war to capture people to sacrifice. They also fought for land.

The Aztecs believed that the jaguar was the bravest of all animals, so the deadliest and most **lethal** Aztec warriors covered their bodies in jaguar skins. They thought that the skins gave them the strength of jaguars during battles.

Eagles were also important to the Aztecs. Fighters wore helmets with birds' beaks, costumes with eagles' wings and had birds' claws attached to their legs. Enemies must have been terrified when jaguar and eagle warriors ran towards them wielding weapons such as bows and arrows.

Aztec warriors who captured a lot of prisoners were given amazing eagle or jaguar costumes.

KILLER FACT!

Aztec warriors had some deadly weapons. The *macahuitl* was a wooden club with a row of razor-sharp blades along the edge. The blades were made from a black stone called obsidian.

The *macahuitl* was an especially lethal Aztec weapon on the battlefield.

City of fear

The Aztecs were cruel but incredibly clever. They built a huge city called Tenochtitlán on a small, muddy island. The city had wide plazas (central meeting places) and many market stalls. By 1500, Tenochtitlán was one of the largest and most impressive cities in the world.

Many Aztec cities were built on sites where previous ancient peoples had lived. The Aztecs built their cities around the **temple pyramids** that were already there. These towering buildings were places where people could worship their gods. The pyramids were also where thousands of unfortunate victims were sacrificed.

The high pyramids must have struck **awe** into people. In Tenochtitlán, the main temple was almost 61 metres (200 feet) high and could be seen above the tall treetops. It was an impressive **symbol** of the Aztecs' power.

This is an illustration of how Tenochtitlán might have looked when the city was at its most powerful. More than 200,000 people lived there.

To celebrate the opening of the biggest temple in Tenochtitlan in 1487, there were four days of celebrations. To honour the temple, thousands of people had their hearts removed while they were still alive.

Victims climbing up Tenochtitlán's main pyramid temple to their doom had to walk past scary serpent sculptures.

CHAPTER 2

Evil emperors

The Aztecs believed that the gods chose their emperor. Their emperor was almost as important and powerful as the gods themselves. But the emperor did not always use this power for good.

The emperor lived in huge, beautiful palaces that showed people how powerful and important he was. He showed off his wealth and power by filling the palaces with guards, hardworking servants and **slaves**.

Ordinary people had to pay the emperor **taxes** and give him things or work for him for free. If they ever saw the emperor, perhaps at a ceremony, they never dared to look into his face or even raise their heads.

An Aztec ruler's palace was very different from the mud and stick homes of ordinary people.

KILLER FACT!

Montezuma, the last Aztec emperor, was so arrogant that he called himself "Emperor of the World". From his huge throne, this ruthless leader ordered the death by sacrifice of thousands of victims.

Emperor Montezuma ruled from a throne carved in the shape of a pyramid. On it were pictures of himself alongside Aztec gods.

Greed and cruelty

People in conquered lands hated the Aztecs not only because of their cruelty, but also because the Aztec emperors demanded a constant supply of gifts, which they called **tributes**, from them. Failure to pay these tributes resulted in nasty punishments.

Conquered peoples were forced to send valuable goods to the Aztecs. Food and items such as jaguar skins, feathered headdresses and gold were given as tributes. Emperors used these tributes to add to the splendour of their palaces.

This is a picture of an Aztec emperor. People were unhappy about being forced to pay tributes to the emperors in order to satisfy their greed.

People who failed to pay their taxes or tributes would be severely punished. Lighter punishments included having homes destroyed or heads shaved. The harshest punishment was death, sometimes by strangling or **stoning**.

DEADLY DID YOU KNOW?

Aztec tribute collectors lived in the conquered regions. They made sure the correct payments were made and were on time. If a person failed to pay, the collector reported him or her to the emperor. The emperor then decided the punishment.

Gold was one of the most valuable items Aztec emperors forced other nations to pay as tributes.

Proof of power

Evil emperors did all they could to strike fear and respect into the hearts of their people.

Emperors wore headdresses and jewellery to show off their power. They also wore them to make themselves look like great warriors and like gods on Earth. Sometimes, the emperors wore things that made them look even scarier. Some had flat discs inserted into their lips that stretched their mouths into frightening sneers.

Emperors ate huge feasts that sometimes included a soup made from human sacrifices.

Sometimes, emperors would eat the remains of victims who had been sacrificed. Body parts were cooked in a kind of human stew. Eating the stew was thought to help the leaders feel a greater connection to the Aztec gods and so give them even more power.

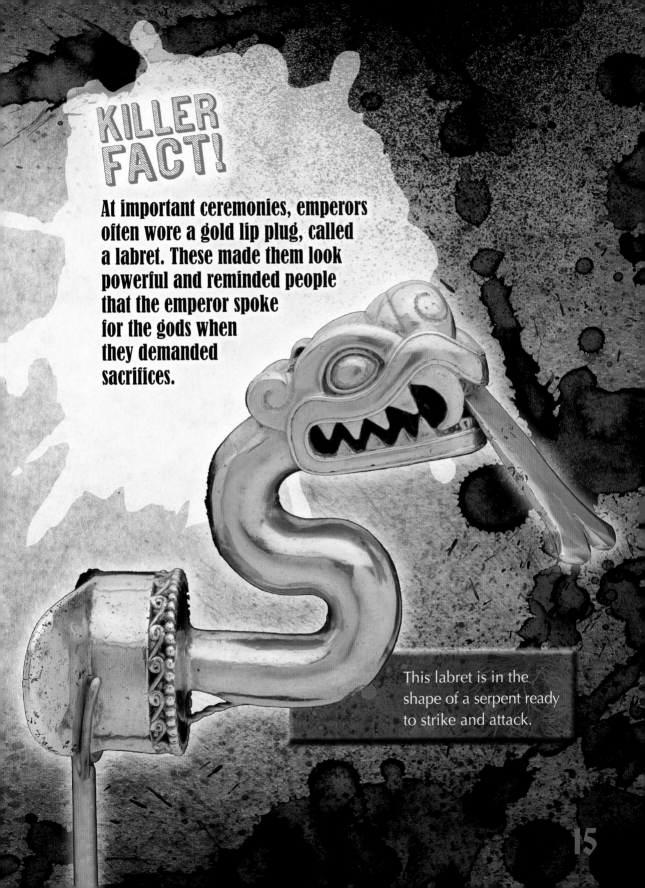

KILLER FACT!

At important ceremonies, emperors often wore a gold lip plug, called a labret. These made them look powerful and reminded people that the emperor spoke for the gods when they demanded sacrifices.

This labret is in the shape of a serpent ready to strike and attack.

CHAPTER 3

Gruesome gods

The Aztecs believed that their gods created the world and that the only way to repay them was with blood. Some gruesome gods even demanded particular body parts. Sacrifices were a way of honouring the gods. **Offerings** of blood were believed to feed the gods and keep them strong when they became tired from looking after the world and its people. Aztecs believed that only by offering the gods blood, could they avoid disaster.

Huehueteotl was the fire god. The Aztecs believed if they did not sacrifice and burn people as offerings to Huehueteotl, their cities would burn down.

Huehueteotl was also the god of old age. He was highly respected because many Aztecs died young.

Vitzilopuestli. Idolo principal delos Mexicanos.

DEADLY DID YOU KNOW?

The Aztecs believed their sun god, Huitzilopochtli, was in a constant struggle with darkness. If the sun god was tired or unhappy, he would refuse to bring out the sun and all the crops would die. Aztecs believed that only blood from fresh human hearts would please Huitzilopochtli.

Huitzilopochtli is usually shown as a hummingbird or as a warrior with armour and a helmet made of hummingbird feathers.

17

The god of rain

Tlaloc was the Aztec god of rain and lightning. Aztec people believed that they could stop Tlaloc getting angry and being cruel by offering him child sacrifices.

When Tlaloc was happy, he brought the rain that helped crops to grow. When he was angry, he caused storms, thunder and lightning.

To please Tlaloc, children were sacrificed once a year. These children often cried as they were led away. The Aztecs believed that these tears would mean that Tlaloc would bless them with rain. If the children did not cry, the adults would hurt them to make them cry.

Tlaloc is a horrific-looking god who is often shown with fearsome sharp teeth.

KILLER FACT!

After children were sacrificed to Tlaloc, they were laid outside the city in a cave that was open to the sky. There, the rain given by Tlaloc in return for their sacrifice would wash over their bodies.

This is the skull of a child who was sacrificed long ago by the Aztecs.

God of the night

Tezcatlipoca was god of the night and its creatures. This terrifying god was believed to use evil magic. Tezcatlipoca is usually shown with a black mirror, through which he saw everything that the Aztec people did and thought.

To honour Tezcatlipoca, each year, priests chose one young, handsome prisoner captured in war. For twelve months, this young man lived in luxury, as if he was Tezcatlipoca himself. After this time, he was honoured with dances and flowers. Then he was forced to climb the steps of a temple. At the top, his heart was removed in a **ritual** sacrifice.

Aztecs believed that mirrors made of polished black obsidian stone would allow the user to see into the underworld, where the dead existed in a world of darkness. Black mirrors were also linked to caves, which were seen as entrances to the underworld.

This turquoise mask **represents** Tezcatlipoca.

The name Tezcatlipoca means "smoking mirror". That is why this Aztec god is often shown with an **obsidian** mirror, like this one, on his chest, in his headdress or replacing his right foot.

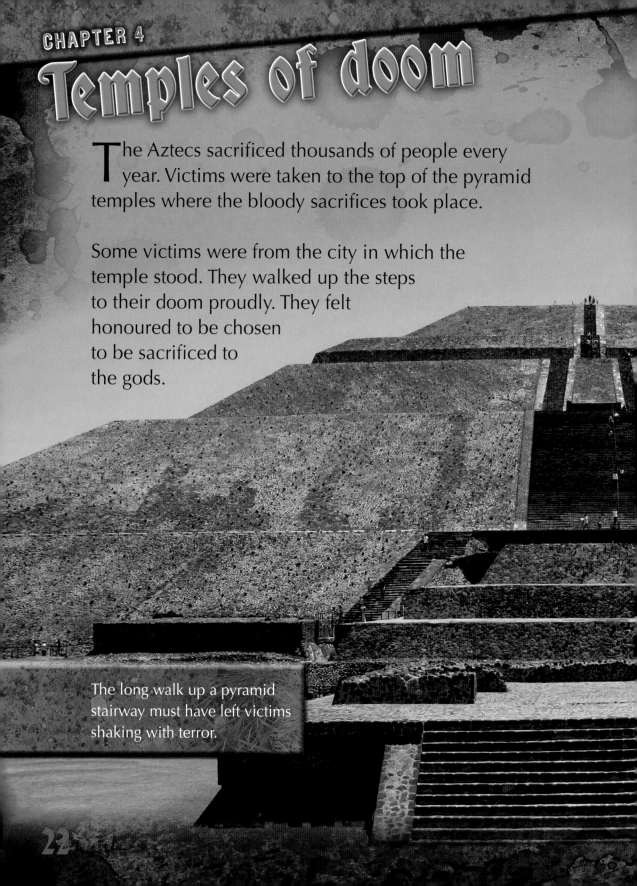

CHAPTER 4

Temples of doom

The Aztecs sacrificed thousands of people every year. Victims were taken to the top of the pyramid temples where the bloody sacrifices took place.

Some victims were from the city in which the temple stood. They walked up the steps to their doom proudly. They felt honoured to be chosen to be sacrificed to the gods.

The long walk up a pyramid stairway must have left victims shaking with terror.

The Aztecs believed that if they were sacrificed it would earn them a place in paradise in the **afterlife**, the life they lived after death.

Most of the people who were sacrificed were enemies who had been captured in battles. They were forced to walk up the stairs of the temple and as they climbed to their deaths, a crowd of people gathered in the square to watch the spectacle.

Sacrificial knives were often decorated to show that they had a special purpose.

KILLER FACT!

Razor-sharp knives were used to kill people. Aztec knives were often made from a stone called flint.

Sites of sacrifice

The sinister sacrifices of unfortunate human victims took place on a flat platform on top of the pyramid temples. The crowds of ordinary Aztecs below could look up and watch the scary scene. After the sacrifice, the victim's lifeless body was rolled down the steps of the pyramid, as people in the square below watched.

Templo del ydolo Vitz puc-tli.

At the bottom of the steps, there were people waiting to cut the body into pieces. Sometimes, if the person sacrificed was an enemy, the warrior who captured him was given the limbs to eat. The stomach and chest were offered to the gods. The skull was removed and displayed on a wooden rack. These racks were huge and stacked up high with the skulls of many other sacrificed dead people.

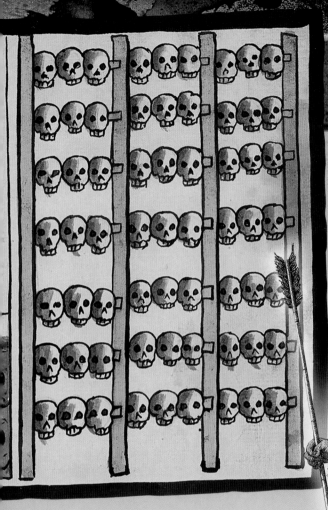

These terrifying towers of skulls showed how many enemies had been killed in war.

DEADLY DID YOU KNOW?
The Aztec emperor Montezuma (right) had a zoo of exotic animals. He fed them the remains of bodies that were thrown down the steps of the temple.

Time to die

The Aztec sacrifices may have been bloodthirsty and brutal, but they were carried out in an orderly fashion. The dates of the ceremonies were marked by calendars carved in stone.

At the centre of the sun stone calendar is the face of the sun god. He holds a human heart in each hand and his long tongue represents a ritual knife. The calendar reminded the Aztec people that only human sacrifice could keep the sun alive.

The sun stone calendar also told the Aztecs when the world might end. So every fifty-two years, they performed the New Fire ceremony and a special sacrifice to prevent disaster.

The sun stone calendar set a schedule for sacrificial deaths.

KILLER FACT!

In the New Fire ceremony, a priest wearing a turquoise mask of the god of fire cut out the heart from a live victim. Then he lit a fire in the victim's chest. If the fire burned brightly, all was well. If not, the Aztecs feared monsters would appear and destroy the world.

Priests wore different masks for the different ceremonies timed by the sun stone calendar.

CHAPTER 5

Sinister ceremonies

Aztec priests offered the gods blood in different ways. In some ceremonies, priests and emperors offered some of their own blood. In others, animals were killed in sacrifice. Human sacrifices struck fear into the hearts of everyone who saw them.

Aztec bloodletting ceremonies usually happened at the end of **elaborate** festivals that lasted for several days. A priest or emperor might prick his ears, tongue, arms or legs with cactus spines, a bone or eagle claws to let out blood.

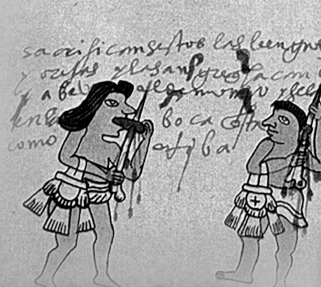

The blood from bloodletting ceremonies, such as those shown here, was often poured over the statues of the gods.

Sometimes, paper was used to soak up the blood. It was then burned to carry the blood to the gods. Bloodletting ceremonies such as this showed the Aztec people that the emperor and priests had the power to feed and please the gods.

KILLER FACT!

During ceremonies, priests wore ornaments in shapes such as a snake with two heads. The snake was a symbol of magical power, and was believed to be deadly. These symbols helped make the priests seem more mysterious and powerful.

During ceremonies, priests wore this double-headed serpent **ornament** on their chest.

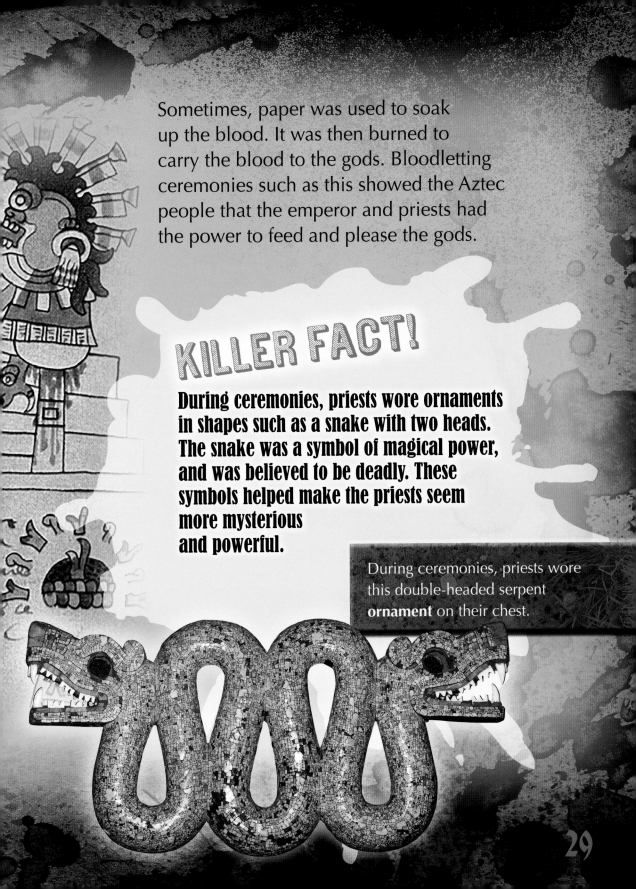

Animal sacrifices

Aztec priests also sacrificed animals in honour of their gods. In many cases, the harder it was to hunt an animal, the more important it was for a sacrifice. A jaguar sacrifice was used for important ceremonies, but this was rare.

Aztecs sacrificed cats, fish, birds and snakes they caught nearby. They also **traded** objects, such as jewellery and pottery, for other sacrificial animals such as quetzals (brightly coloured birds). They even traded for crocodiles from hundreds of kilometres away!

The god Quetzalcóatl was believed to have contributed to the creation of mankind, so making sacrifices to him was very important.

Often, specific animals were linked to particular gods and ceremonies. For example, Quetzalcóatl was a god whose name meant "feathered serpent". When the Aztecs worshipped him, they usually sacrificed butterflies and hummingbirds in his honour.

This illustration shows Aztec priests making offerings to the gods to try to prevent a **drought**.

DEADLY DID YOU KNOW?

In the Aztec capital city of Tenochtitlan, archaeologists discovered more than four hundred different types of animal that had been sacrificed and buried there as offerings to the gods.

Human sacrifices

Masks were an important part of all Aztec ceremonies, especially sacrifices. Some masks were made for display around the temple. During human sacrifices, the priests often wore masks that made them look terrifying!

Priests usually wore masks that made them look like the god they were honouring. For example, the masks created for the god Quetzalcóatl usually had snakes on them.

Masks were designed to make ordinary Aztecs fear the priests who wore them.

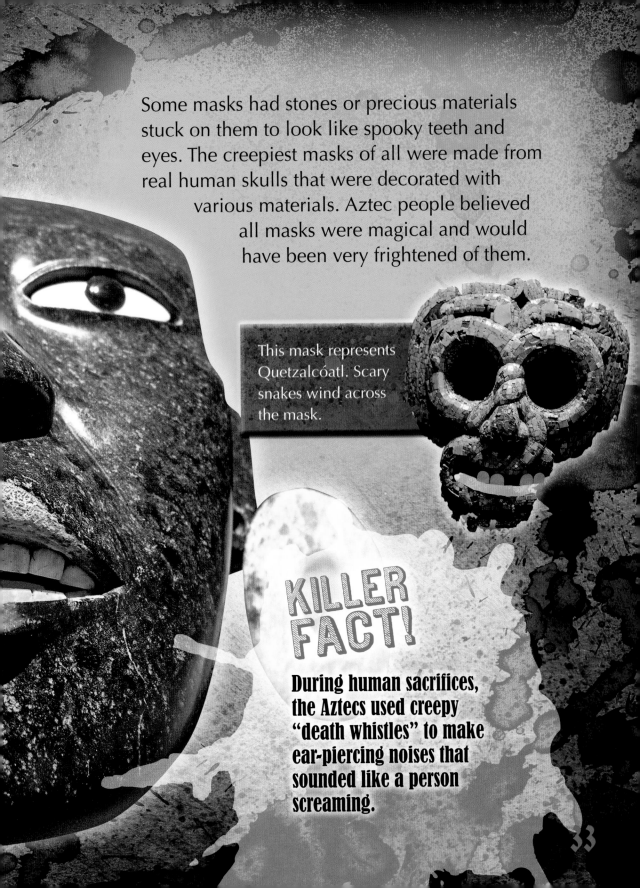

Some masks had stones or precious materials stuck on them to look like spooky teeth and eyes. The creepiest masks of all were made from real human skulls that were decorated with various materials. Aztec people believed all masks were magical and would have been very frightened of them.

This mask represents Quetzalcóatl. Scary snakes wind across the mask.

KILLER FACT!

During human sacrifices, the Aztecs used creepy "death whistles" to make ear-piercing noises that sounded like a person screaming.

CHAPTER 6

Life after death

The Aztecs believed in a life after death. They believed that after a person died, that person lived a different life in another world.

For the Aztecs, the world of the afterlife was arranged in thirteen layers of heavens and nine of the **underworld**. The fate of the dead was determined on the basis of how this person died. For example, all who drowned went to one particular layer of heaven.

This picture shows the deepest layer of the underworld: Mictlan. It was a very dark and very frightening place.

Most ordinary Aztec people who died were believed to go to Mictlan, the deepest layer of the underworld. This was where the terrifying Mictlantecuhtli, the lord of the land of the dead, lived.

KILLER FACT!

The Aztecs believed Mictlantecuhtli was a tall, blood-spattered skeleton with eyeballs in his skull. Sometimes, he wore a necklace of human eyeballs and ear ornaments made from human bones.

Carvings of Mictlantecuhtli often show him standing in a threatening pose, ready to tear apart the dead as they enter his world.

A deadly journey

Aztec people who died ordinary deaths were thought to spend the first four years of their afterlife travelling to Mictlan. Once there, these people spent the rest of their afterlife serving Mictlantecuhtli and living in total darkness.

The journey through the different levels of the underworld to Mictlan was filled with horror. The dead had to cross a path full of snakes and an area with winds that were so strong and sharp that they slashed skin like a knife.

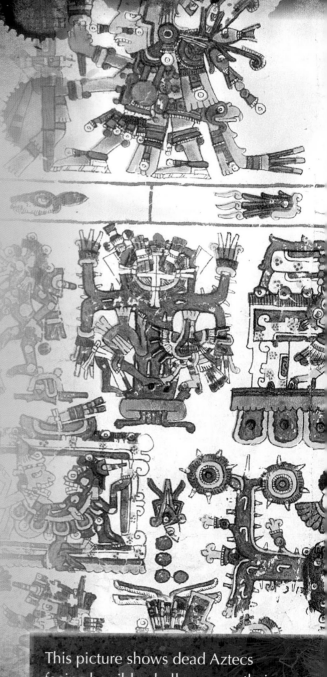

This picture shows dead Aztecs facing horrible challenges on their journeys through the underworld.

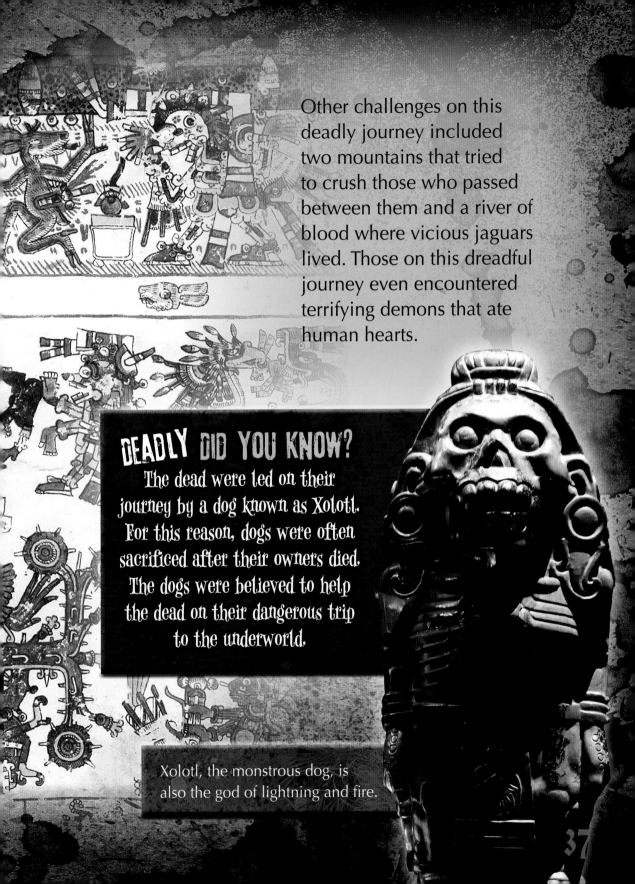

Other challenges on this deadly journey included two mountains that tried to crush those who passed between them and a river of blood where vicious jaguars lived. Those on this dreadful journey even encountered terrifying demons that ate human hearts.

DEADLY DID YOU KNOW?

The dead were led on their journey by a dog known as Xolotl. For this reason, dogs were often sacrificed after their owners died. The dogs were believed to help the dead on their dangerous trip to the underworld.

Xolotl, the monstrous dog, is also the god of lightning and fire.

Death rituals

Aztecs who died a natural death, perhaps from old age, were buried with objects to help them when they reached the underworld. They were also buried with gifts, to please the terrifying god Mictlantecuhtli and his wife when they reached Mictlan.

If an ordinary Aztec died, the family kept the body for 80 days before it was buried. This gave the family time to say goodbye. Then the body was dressed and a **jade** stone placed under the tongue. After this, the body was often cremated (burned).

The Aztecs cremated their dead in special ceremonies.

The remains were then buried with everything the dead person needed for the journey to Mictlan. This included food, drink, clothes, valuables and tools. Even weapons were buried to help the dead fight the monsters they would meet along the way to the underworld.

KILLER FACT!

After bodies were burned, the ashes were put into a vase that was buried in a deep hole beneath the family home.

Aztec funeral vases were often shaped like scary gods or wild animals.

A painful death

Some religions state that what happens to you after death depends on how good a life you have lived. For the Aztecs, the only thing that mattered was the way a person died – and the best death was horrible and painful.

Most of those who died a violent death went to an Aztec heaven or paradise in their afterlife. One layer there was for victims of sacrifice, another for warriors and others killed in war, and another for women who died giving birth to their children.

This picture shows the death of an Aztec man who has offered himself for sacrifice. The Aztecs believed that death by sacrifice was an honour.

The job that people were given in their afterlife depended on how they died, too. In the afterlife, warriors who died in battle or were captured and sacrificed had the job of helping the sun god lift up the sun each morning. Women who died giving birth helped the sun god bring down the sun again in the evening.

DEADLY DID YOU KNOW?

It is said after helping the sun god for four years, dead warriors were transformed into hummingbirds and butterflies.

Masks of death

When an Aztec emperor died, a death mask was made for him to wear. The Aztecs believed that these strange, sinister-looking masks would bring the emperor back to life again, in the afterlife.

Death masks were made of precious materials and usually placed over the dead emperor's face. Death masks were often made to look like a god's face. Along with the mask, the dead person was also sometimes dressed in the clothing of a particular god.

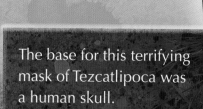

The base for this terrifying mask of Tezcatlipoca was a human skull.

A death mask usually had closed eyes and an open mouth. Some masks were buried alongside a body or with an emperor's ashes. Sometimes a family kept the death mask on display, as a chilling reminder of the power of their dead ruler.

KILLER FACT!

Gold was an important precious material used by Aztec mask-makers. Gold was special because Aztecs believed it was the sun's faeces.

Only very important Aztecs wore death masks made of precious materials such as turquoise.

Death of an empire

The Aztec empire ended in the way it had first grown into a huge and successful power – through bloody and deadly violence.

The Spanish invader Hernán Cortés had heard tales of Aztec treasures and sailed from Europe to conquer the Empire. Montezuma II was the Aztec Empire's last ruler. When the Spanish arrived in 1519, he gave Hernán Cortés gifts of gold, but Cortés wanted more.

The Aztecs fought bravely against the Spanish invaders but were overcome by their superior weapons and battle skills.

Cortés persuaded the tribes who no longer wanted to pay tributes to Montezuma to help his men attack and take over the city of Tenochtitlán. Cortés then travelled around the Empire stealing gold, killing people who tried to resist and destroying Aztec temples and treasures. The Aztec Empire was over.

DEADLY DID YOU KNOW?

The Spanish also brought with them a deadly disease called smallpox, so many of those Aztecs who survived the Spanish invasion were killed off by disease instead. Millions of Aztecs died from this fatal infection.

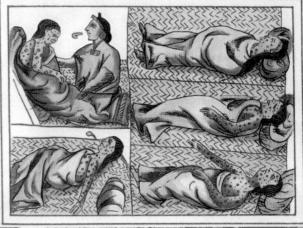

This picture shows Aztecs suffering and dying from smallpox.

Glossary

afterlife life after death. Some people believe that after we die we go to live in another world.

arrogant full of a sense of self-importance

awe amazement and wonder

civilization settled community in which people live together and use systems, such as writing, to communicate

conquer use force to take over a city or country

drought period of time with little or no rainfall

elaborate detailed

emperor male leader or ruler of an empire

empire large area of land or group of countries ruled over by one leader

faeces digestive waste

fatal resulting in death

jade precious green stone

lethal deadly

obsidian hard, dark, glass-like volcanic rock

offerings things that people give as part of a religious ceremony or ritual

ornaments decorative objects

prey animal that is caught and eaten by other animals

priests religious leaders

pyramids tall buildings with a square or rectangular base and stepped or layered sides. Unlike Egyptian pyramids, Aztec pyramids had a flat base at the top, not a point.

resented unhappy or angry about something

ritual ceremony performed for religious reasons

ruthless having no mercy

sacrifice animal or human killed to honour a god or gods

slaves people who are owned by other people and have to obey them

stoning killing a person by throwing stones at him or her

symbol sign for something

taxes money paid to a ruler or a government

temple building that people go to in order to worship their god or gods

traded bought, sold and exchanged goods

transformed dramatically changed

tribes groups of people who live together

tributes gifts of food and other items paid by people to their ruler

underworld mythical world of the dead

Find out more

Books

Angry Aztecs (Horrible Histories), Terry Deary (Scholastic, 2016)

Aztec (Eyewitness), DK (DK Children, 2011)

Aztec and Maya (Hands-on History!), Fiona MacDonald (Armadillo Books, 2015)

The Aztec Empire (You Choose: Historical Eras), Elizabeth Raum (Raintree, 2015)

DKfindout! Maya, Incas and Aztecs, DK (DK Children, 2018)

Websites

www.bbc.com/bitesize/clips/zxmxpv4
Learn more about the Aztec Empire.

www.dkfindout.com/uk/history/aztecs
Find out more about the Aztecs.

Index